Cooking with My Mother:

Six Illustrated Classic Chinese and Vietnamese Recipes

Alan Y. Jen

ISBN: 9798321744420

DEDICATION

I dedicate this book to my mother,
from whom I have learned more than recipes:

Chin Sieou Jen (Chinese name)
Cam Tu Hong (maiden name in Vietnamese)

June 08 1970: Taipei, Taiwan

Table of Contents

Chapter 1 About My Mother

My mother has a unique background. She was exposed to both Chinese and Vietnamese cuisine because she was born and raised in Hanoi, Vietnam, with ethnic Chinese parents from the Fujian province of China.

Back in her parents' era, it was common that only the eldest son inherited the family fortune. Those who were not the eldest son sometimes chose to emigrate overseas. In 1911, my maternal grandfather at age 4 emigrated with his uncle (both not eldest sons) to Hanoi, Vietnam, where later my grandparents married and my mother was born. My mother grew up with 8 siblings in Hanoi, and food had always been central to family gatherings.

As part of the Geneva Accords in 1954, the Communists came to power in North Vietnam, which included Hanoi. After less than one year under Communists rule, her family felt the future for the family business was bleak. For example, the Communists decided to tax all business inventory, and business owners like my mother's family had to pay tax based on the amount of inventory regardless of the amount of sales. Her family made the difficult decision to abandon the family business and moved to the Cholon neighborhood of Saigon in South Vietnam on March 29 1955.

In the 1960's, my mother was introduced to my would-be father in a long-distance relationship between Vietnam and Taiwan, Republic of China. This chanced introduction was the result of my mother's best friend in Vietnam dating my father's best friend in Taiwan. When the best friends decided to tie the knot, my mother accompanied her best friend to Taiwan. Within 15 days of spending time together, my mother and father married too.

My parents in Taiwan in 1968

My mother making pho

My mother and father both worked, with my mother's work commute being 1.5-hour each direction. So, my father cooked almost all weeknights. We were treated to my father's cooking from northern China, his birthplace. On the weekend, my mother would cook recipes from her childhood, which were a treat to both my brother and me, because those dishes were not every day dishes you could find in Taiwan.

My entire family emigrated to the United States in the early 1980's, where my brother and I went to grammar school and middle school. Now fast forward almost forty years. I retired. At that time, I decided to learn my mother's recipes as a way to relive my childhood as well as to cook for her in her old age.

When learning my mother's recipes, I carefully documented all steps in writing, including taking pictures of ingredients that were not easily found in the United States. Additionally, whenever my mother said to put in "a handful" or "a bit" of such and such ingredient, I would attempt to quantify the amount so the recipes can be repeated consistently. I would iterate with different quantities – 1 tablespoon this time, 1 teaspoon the next time – until the outcome received my mother's stamp-of-approval.

This book consists of my mother's recipes -- six classic Chinese and Vietnamese dishes.

Chapter 2 Getting the Most out of the Book

I describe this book as "illustrated" because I include many photos. They are meant to help you visually identify the right ingredients and compare during the cooking process to ensure you are on the right track.

My mother took the liberty to use more ingredients she preferred, for example, more shrimps in pan fried rice sticks. These choices were meant to enhance flavor. These recipes do take time to prepare and cook as well as being delicious. Feel free to use these recipes as baseline and adjust to your liking, both in taste and time required.

I wish you success in the journey of learning and enjoying these six classic Chinese and Vietnamese recipes. Bon Appetit!

Chinese Sausage (also known as Chinese Style Sausage). My mother highly recommends the brand shown in the photo: "Kam Yen Jan".

In Chapter 9, I present each less common ingredient in glossary format with photos of both the packaging and the content whenever applicable. Often the photos include the name of the ingredient in English, Chinese, and Vietnamese. That way, it will be easier to identify them.

When you are ready to try out a recipe for the first time in Chapters 3 to 8, I recommend reading all sections of that recipe beforehand. You may have opportunities to break down the steps over several days if you have other time commitments.

Here is a breakdown of the sections of each recipe.

6 BEEF PHO

越南牛肉河粉 | phở bò

I present the recipe name and a photo of the final outcome. I even include the recipe name in English, Chinese, and Vietnamese, in case you come across them in different situations and want to compare.

Start to Finish

- Preparation: 30 minutes
- Chilling: at least 2 hours
- Cooking: 1.5 hours

Then, I show the estimated preparation, chilling, and cooking times. When a recipe calls for chilling one or more uncooked or cooked ingredients, consider your other time commitments and decide whether to chill overnight or over the next several hours.

Makes

- 6 servings

I then list the number of servings in entrée size portion for adults.

Ingredients

- 2.25 lbs. beef stew cubes
- 2 teaspoons of salt
- 1 teaspoon of pepper
- 1 teaspoon of soy sauce
- 1 bunch of green onion
- 1 bunch of cilantros
- 1 medium white onion
- 14 oz of pho
- 4 cups of beef broth from a cartoon or cans

The list of ingredients follows. I highly recommend cross referencing the ingredients with the Chapter 9 ingredients glossary.

Finally, I list the steps, showing photos of critical steps (such as how to fold a spring roll).

Occasionally, I give tips after the steps section.

Chapter 3 Sticky Rice

糯米飯 (油飯) | XÔI MẶN

Start to Finish

- Preparation: 1 hour
- Chilling: 1 hour
- Cooking: 1 hour after chilling

Makes

- 6 servings

Ingredients

- 3.5 oz dried shrimps
- 1.2 ounces dried mushrooms
- 1 teaspoon of soy sauce
- 4 cups chicken broth
- 7 oz or 5 Chinese sausages
- 2 cups of uncooked sweet rice
- 1/4 cup and 2 tablespoons of cooking oil
- 1/2 cup chopped onion
- Peanuts (optional). Soak in water to get rid of any skins

Commentary

- This dish is served at one-month birthday of a baby, and commonly given to extended family along with red dyed hard-boiled eggs.

Steps

1. Wash dried mushrooms with water to rid of any dirt. Soak in water at a level that barely immerses them for at least an hour in the refrigerator -- place the dried mushroom with the stalk side down in the water because that is the toughest part. Save the soaking water for later.

2. Wash dried shrimps to rid of any dirt. Soak in water at a level that barely immerses them for at least an hour in the refrigerator. Save the soaking water for later use.

3. Pour out the soaking water from the soaking bowls of dried mushrooms and dried shrimps into a measuring cup with 2 cups capacity.
4. Wring out excess water from each mushroom into the measuring cup. Slice each mushroom into bite size (approximately 0.25" wide and 0.5" to 0.75" long). Dispose of stalks.

5. Wring out any water from dried shrimps into the measuring cup. Then use a small knife to get rid of any visible veins, and cut into two to three chunks for each dried shrimp.

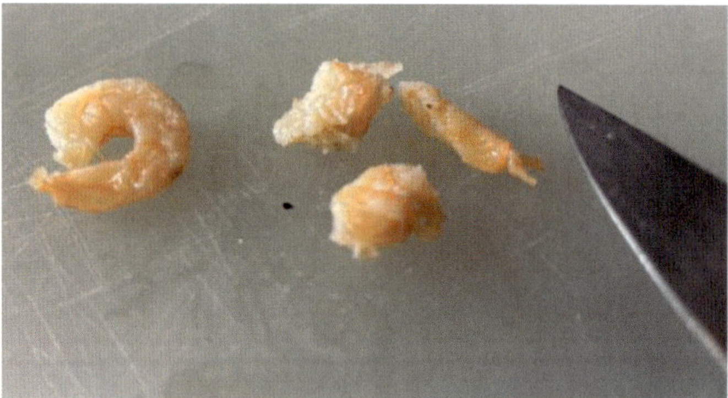

6. Add the soy sauce to the measuring cup. This liquid mixture should measure about 0.75 to 1 cup.
7. Slice Chinese sausages into thin cross-sectional slices, separating from the casing. *Tip: The easiest way to remove Chinese sausage from the casing is to slice the entire Chinese sausage link, then separate the slices from the casing (it is too cumbersome to cut off one slice, separate that slice from the casing, cut another slice, separate that second slice from the casing, etc.).*

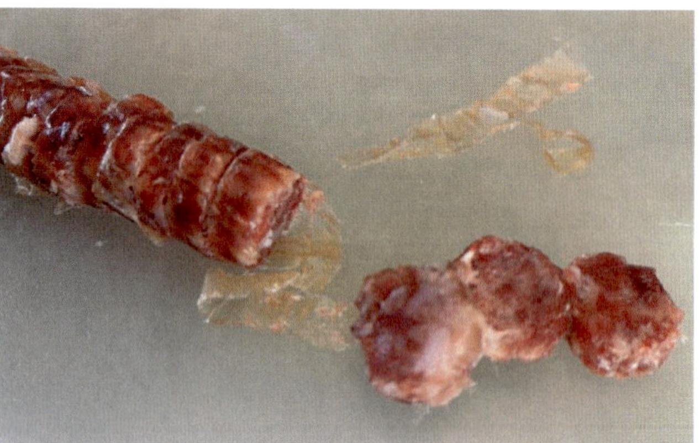

8. Pan fry chopped onion in 1/4 cup of cooking oil in a pan on medium heat until early signs of yellowing (note that chopped onion will continue to brown some more after removing from the heat). Remove from heat and put aside until serving.

9. In the same pan, sauté Chinese sausages in existing oil until golden red on medium heat. Set aside.

10. In the same pan, sauté sliced dried mushrooms and dried shrimps on medium heat until cooked. Leave them in the pan.
11. Add to the pan 2 tablespoons of cooking oil. Stir in the sweet rice to coat well with the cooking oil. Then pour in all the liquid from the measuring cup to the pan. After the rice absorbs the liquid, start periodically add the chicken broth – about half a cup at a time – to the pan as the rice absorbs the chicken broth. Stir frequently to prevent the sweet rice from sticking to the bottom of the pan.
12. After adding the last bit of chicken broth, cover to cook for about 10 to 12 more minutes on low to medium heat -- stir every few minutes to prevent the sweet rice from sticking to the bottom of the pan. When the sweet rice is cooked, add cooked sliced sausage. Add optional peanuts. Mix well.

13. Place the cooked dish from the pan onto plates, then sprinkle chopped onion on top to serve.

Chapter 4 Pan Fried Rice Stick Noodles

炒米粉 | bún gạo xào chay

Start to Finish

- Preparation: 1 hour
- Cooking: 1 hour

Makes

- 6 servings

Ingredients

- A total of 16 oz of vegetables

a) 8 to 12 oz sugar peas

b) 4 to 6 oz carrots

- 7 oz Chinese sausage (5 sausage links)
- 7 oz Hsin-Chu rice stick, the thin kind
- 1 lb. shrimps, any size between 21/25 to 41/50 (23 shrimps of 21/25 size), deveined and shell removed
- 2 cups of chicken broth
- 1 teaspoon soy sauce
- 0.75 cup of water
- Optional: 1 bunch green onion or scallion. Chopped in half-inch chunks

Steps

1. Wash the sugar peas. Peel threads from both ends of each pod. Cut each pod into bite size chunks.

2. Wash the carrots. Cut off and dispose the ends. Then use a peeler to peel off and dispose the skin. Use a peeler to shred the core into pieces. Use a pair of clean scissors to cut up into bite size, under 1 inch in length.

3. Slice Chinese sausages into thin cross-sectional slices, separating from the casing. *Tip: The easiest way to remove Chinese sausage from the casing is to slice the entire Chinese sausage link, then separate the slices from the casing (it is too cumbersome to cut off one slice, separate that slice from the casing, cut another slice, separate that second slice from the casing, etc.).*

4. Immerse and soak Hsin-Chu rice stick in lukewarm water for about 8 minutes. Drain and wring out most of the water from the Hsin-Chu rice stick – it does not need to be completely dry or soft.

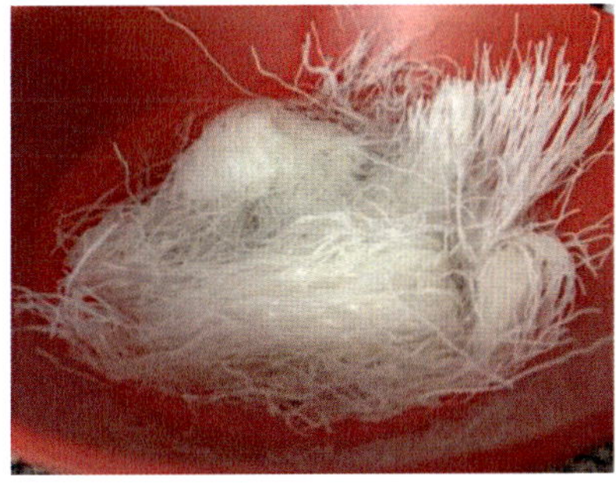

5. The next 3 steps can be done sequentially or concurrently.
    a. Use a pan with 2 tablespoons of oil to cook the raw whole shrimps. Cook the shrimps on both sides until cooked on medium heat, about 3 minutes each side. Put aside the cooked whole shrimps. Chop up into small chunks -- I find it easier to use a fork to hold each cooked shrimp in place while using a knife to cut between the tines of the fork.

    b. In order to preserve the taste of vegetables, pan fry in a second pan with 2 tablespoons of oil sugar peas and shredded carrots until cooked. This takes about 8 to 10 minutes on medium heat. Remove the pan from the heat when cooked.

    c. In order to preserve the taste of Chinese sausage slices, pan fry them in a third pan with about 2 tablespoons of oil. Put aside on a plate or bowl once golden red. Save this pan along with the oil.

6. Create a cooking mixture by combining the chicken broth, soy sauce, and water.
7. In the same pan where Chinese sausage was cooked, add Hsin-Chu rice stick to coat well in the existing oil left from cooking the Chinese sausages. Periodically add cooking mixture about half a cup of at a time until the Hsin-Chu rice stick is semi soft.

8. After all the cooking mixture is added and the moisture is mostly gone from the rice sticks but not completely dry, add Chinese sausage and shrimps. Mix well -- it may be necessary to use a clean pair of scissors to cut the rice stick into shorter lengths so all ingredients can mix well together. Then, add sugar peas and carrots. Turn off heat once the above ingredients are mixed with the rice sticks and are heated up (as these ingredients have cooled down while being put aside).

9. Mix in optional chopped green onion or scallion.

10. Put on plates to serve.

Tip

Feel free to experiment on the size of “slices” and “chunks” of sugar peas, carrots, shrimps, Chinese sausage, and green onion. They should be smaller than bite size so that you will be able to enjoy more than one ingredient in each bite.

Chapter 5 Spring Rolls

春捲 | CHẢ GIÒ

Start to Finish

- Preparation: 1 hour
- Chilling: at least 2 hours
- Cooking: 1 hour before chilling. 0.5 hour after chilling

Makes

- 25 spring rolls. 4 to 6 servings if served as an entrée.

Ingredients

- Approximately 29 oz of vegetables:
    - 10-14 oz sugar peas
    - 5-7 oz carrots
    - 10-12 oz of bean sprouts. Mung bean sprouts preferred
- 3 oz of vermicelli
- 1 lb. shrimps, any size between 21/25 to 41/50 (23 shrimps of 21/25 size), deveined and shell removed
- 11 oz. of ground pork
- 1 teaspoon soy sauce
- 2 eggs
- 25 spring roll pastry sheets
- 1 head of iceberg lettuce
- 2 to 3 oz perilla leaves. May be substituted by mint leaves

Dipping Sauce

- 4 tablespoons fish sauce
- 3 cloves of garlic. Finely chopped
- 1 tablespoon vinegar
- 14 tablespoons water
- 1.5 tablespoons sugar

Steps

1. Make the dipping sauce by combining all the sauce ingredients. The sauce can be refrigerated for future use. If you wish to adjust the dipping sauce more to your liking, try out by dipping with a clean finger (if you taste by "drinking" it, the flavor is too strong).

   - If the dipping sauce is too sweet, add more vinegar.
   - If too bitter, add more sugar.
   - If too diluted, add more fish sauce.
   - If too strong, add more water.

2. Wash the sugar peas. Peel threads from both ends of each pod. Chop finely or use a food processor to shred the sugar peas. It may be necessary to pass through a second time to shred them.

3. Wash the carrots. Cut off and dispose the ends. Then use a peeler to peel off and dispose the skin. Next peel the core into thin slices. Finally chop finely or use a food processor to shred the carrot slices. It's perfectly fine to mix together sugar peas and carrots.

4. Wash the bean sprouts.
5. Soak vermicelli in lukewarm water to the point of being soft, approximately 12 minutes. Drain and wring out water so that water is not dripping from it. Use a pair of clean scissors to cut the vermicelli into bite size, approximately 0.5 to 1 inch in length.

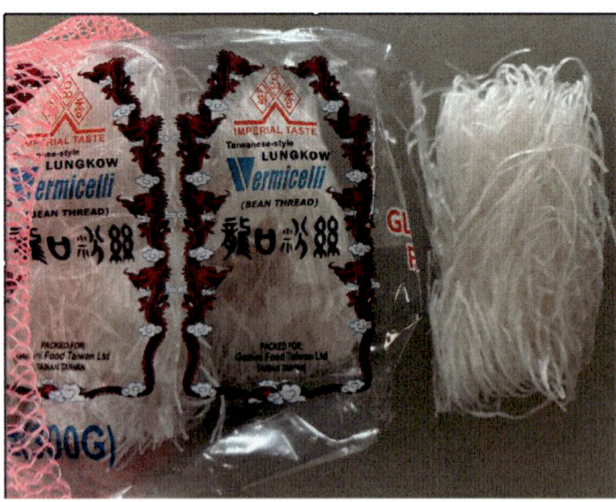

6. Pan fry the raw whole shrimps in about 2 tablespoons of oil. Cook the shrimps on both sides until cooked on medium heat, about 3 minutes each side. Put aside the cooked whole shrimps. Chop up into small chunks -- I find it easier to use a fork to hold each cooked shrimp in place while using a knife to cut between the tines of the fork.

7. In a bowl, mix the ground pork with soy sauce, egg yolks. Save the egg whites in a separate bowl.

8. Cook the ground pork in the same pan that was used to cook the shrimps. Use a spatula to press the ground pork to avoid clumping. When the ground pork is fully cooked, add bean sprouts to the pan; stir frequently to cook until soft. Add the sugar peas and carrots; stir frequently to cook until soft. Add vermicelli; stir frequently to cook until soft. Add chopped shrimps. Mix well all ingredients. Add oil as needed throughout.

9. At this point, all filler ingredients are cooked and mixed together. It is important to allow the filler ingredients to chill before wrapping; otherwise, the moisture that evaporates from them may make the spring roll pastry sheets too mushy to hold together. Refrigerate at least 2 hours.
10. Roll the spring rolls. (a) Place a spring roll pastry sheet in rhombus shape on a cutting board or a plate. (b) Place the filler ingredients in the bottom half of the sheet, leaving space on both right and left sides. (c) Tightly tuck the sheet under the filling on the top side. (d) Roll into a cylinder up to about half way from the bottom. (e) At this point, fold from both left and right sides. (f) Wrap tightly to near the top of the rhombus, then seal with egg whites.

As you finish rolling a spring roll, place each one with the sealing side down so the spring roll holds together even better as you roll more of them. This can be refrigerated until you are ready to pan fry to serve.

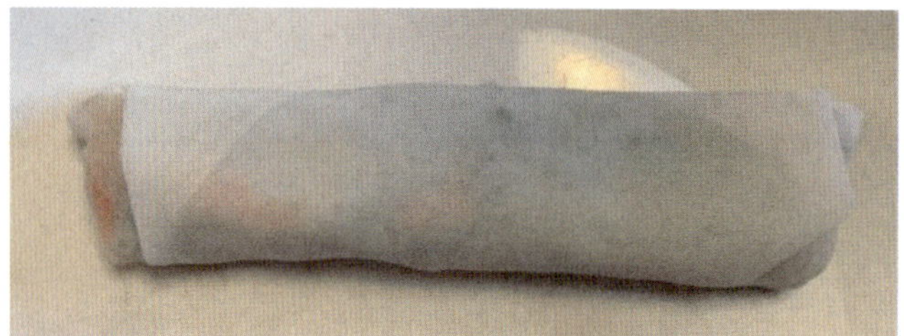

11. Pan fry with sufficient oil the wrapped spring rolls with the sealing side down to help keep each spring roll in one piece. Rotate on all sides to make evenly golden brown. Add oil as needed. *Note: Spring rolls taste best when freshly fried. Pan fry only the spring rolls you plan to eat for the current meal, while refrigerating the rest to pan fry at future meal times.*

12. Wash iceberg lettuce and perilla. Take the iceberg lettuce leaves off the core. Take perilla leaves of the stem.

13. Serve with dipping sauce, iceberg lettuce, and perilla. I like to use a pair of clean scissors to cut each spring roll into 4 pieces (or alternate bite size) so they are ready to be eaten on the plate.

Chapter 6 Beef Pho

越南牛肉河粉 | phở bò

Start to Finish

- Preparation: 30 minutes
- Chilling: at least 2 hours
- Cooking: 1.25 hour before chilling. 0.5 hour after chilling

Makes

- 4 servings

Ingredients

- 2 lbs. beef stew cubes
- 2 teaspoons of salt
- 1 teaspoon of pepper
- 1 bunch of green onion
- 1 bunch of cilantros
- 1 medium white onion
- 14 oz of pho
- 4 cups of beef broth from a cartoon or cans. I recommend low sodium beef broth because you can always season to taste later.

Commentary

This differs from the beef pho that you would get at restaurants, where the beef is thinly sliced and beautifully placed on top to show the appearance of a large amount of beef. My mother calls that "restaurant presentation style". The below recipe, which my mother calls "home cooking style", consists of more volume of beef in the form of beef cube chunks. More flavor per bite!

Steps

1. The store-bought beef stew cubes may be bigger than bite size. Cut each beef stew cube into bite size chunks. Sprinkle and rub in salt and pepper.

2. Fill a pot with 4 cups of water and beef chunks – if the beef is not fully immersed in water, add more water until barely fully immersed. Bring the water to a boil on medium heat while covered. Then simmer on low to medium heat while covered for one hour.

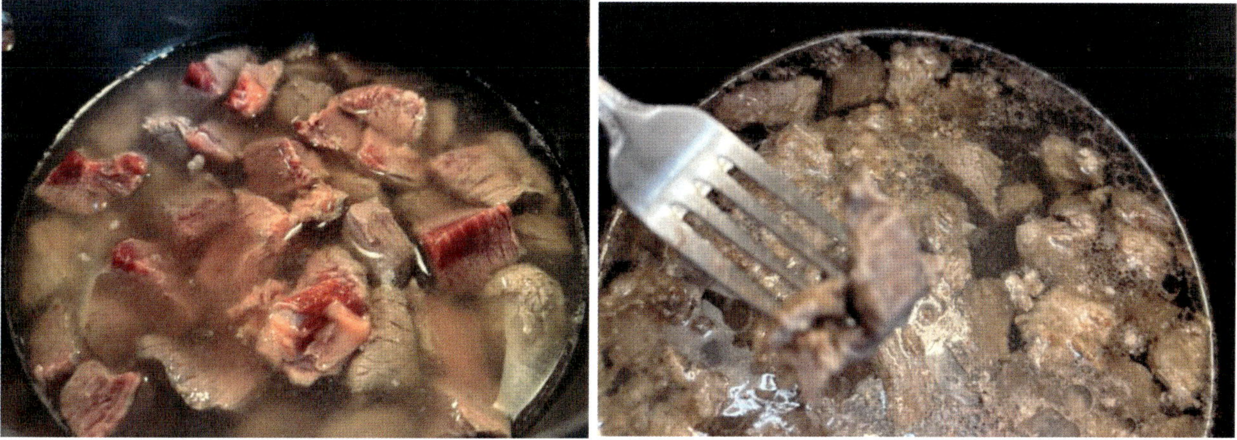

3. After the pot of beef and hot water cools down, refrigerate the pot in the refrigerator for at least 2 hours.
4. Chop the green onion in about 0.25" chunks; you may wish to use spice scissors to do this.

5. Take the leaves off cilantro; discard the stem. Chop the cilantro; you may wish to use spice scissors to do this.

6. Discard the skin from the white onion. Chop and discard the top and bottom parts of the white onion. Slice the white onion in thin circular slices from top to bottom; you may wish to use a mandoline slicer – perform this step by following the directions in the mandoline slicer manual. Separate out the onion pieces.

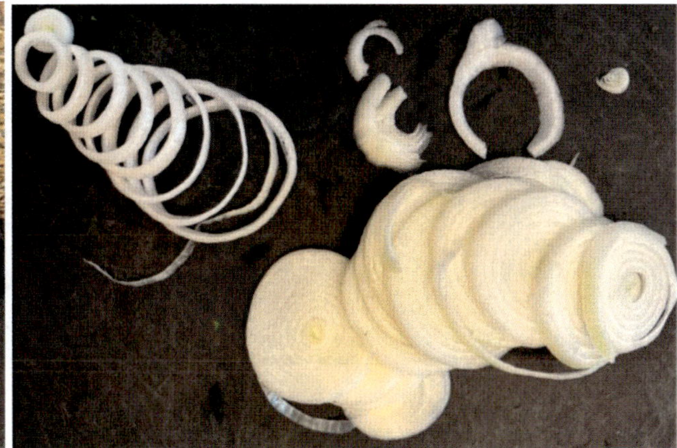

7. Perform these two steps concurrently:

- Put 16 cups of water in a pot. Bring the water to boiling while covered, then add the pho in the boiling water. Cook the pho uncovered on medium heat until cooked, about 20 minutes – stir and add more water to the pot if the pho starts to stick to the bottom of the pot. The pho is fully cooked when soft without becoming mushy. Afterwards, rinse with cold water in a pasta strainer.

- Take out the pot with beef from the refrigerator. Skin off the top layer of fat. Combine the 4 cups of beef broth from a cartoon or cans with the existing liquid in the pot. Start heating this pot at the moment when pho is put in the other pot. Bring this pot to a boil on medium to high heat while covered. Then simmer covered on low to medium heat until ready to serve in the next step.

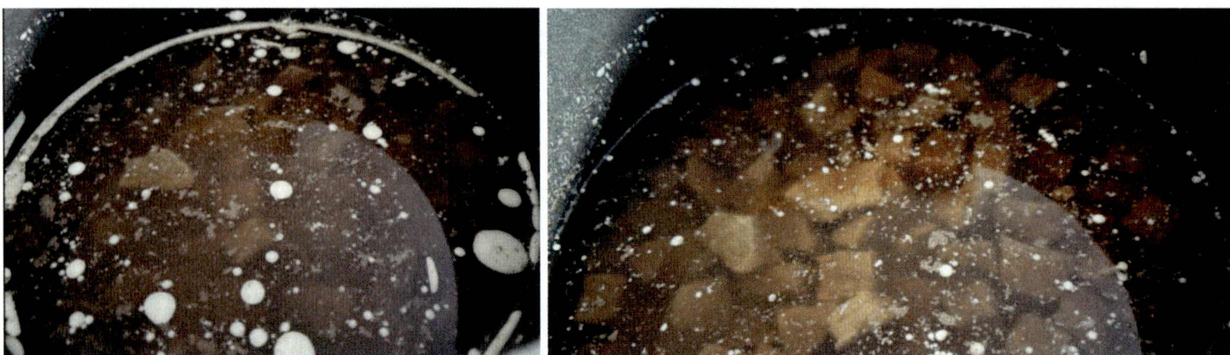

8. Season to taste the beef broth. To serve, place pho at the bottom of a bowl, topped with raw green onion, cilantro, and white onion. Then add to the bowl broth and beef. The broth should completely cover the pho and raw vegetables. The beef does not need to be completely covered by the broth as the beef was already heated up.

Chapter 7 Sticky Rice with Chinese Sausage

臘腸糯米飯 (臘腸油飯) | Xôi Lạp Xưởng

Start to Finish

- Preparation: 15 minutes
- Cooking: 1 hour

Makes

- 8 servings

Ingredients

- 2 cups of sweet rice
- 7 oz or 5 Chinese sausages

Steps

1. Diagonally slice Chinese sausages, separating from the casing. *Tip: The easiest way to remove Chinese sausage from the casing is to slice the entire Chinese sausage link, then separate the slices from the casing (it is too cumbersome to cut off one slice, separate that slice from the casing, cut another slice, separate that second slice from the casing, etc.).*

2. Cook sweet rice with 5 cups of water in a covered pot on medium to high heat until boiling, about 4-6 minutes. Then simmer covered until water is evaporated from the pot (no visible water, only moisture), about 20-25 minutes. At that time, place Chinese sausage slices on top of the sweet rice in the covered pot while continuing to simmer until the sweet rice is cooked (about 5 additional minutes).

3. Once sweet rice is fully cooked, remove and put aside the Chinese sausage slices.
4. Best served hot. Serve with steamed sweet rice on the bottom and Chinese sausage slices on the top.

Chapter 8 Mung Bean Coated Sticky Rice

綠豆糯米飯 | XÔI VÒ

Start to Finish

- Preparation: 5 minutes
- Chilling: 2 hours or overnight
- Cooking: 0.5 hour before chilling, 0.5 hour after chilling

Makes

- 4 servings

Ingredients:

- 0.75 cups of dried peeled mung beans
- 1 cups of sweet rice
- 1 cup of dried chopped onion flakes
- ½ cup of cooking oil

Steps:

1. Sift dried peeled mung beans in cold water to rid of any dirt and dust. Do this very briefly to avoid losing the scent of beans.
2. Cook the washed beans in a covered pot with 1.33 cups of water on medium heat until boiling in about 4-5 minutes – watch closely to prevent the water from boiling over the pot. Then turn down the heat to simmer until cooked in about 30 additional minutes. Verify that beans are cooked such that the beans can be pressed like chunkier version of mashed potato. Press with the back of a large spoon to turn the beans into a paste. Refrigerate for 2 or more hours.

   If the cooked beans are too dry or under cooked, add more water to cook more. If too much water still remains in the pot, cook more time until the water is no longer visible. It's ok to have moisture just not watery.

3. Cook sweet rice with 2.5 cups of water in a covered pot. Start on medium to high heat until boiling, about 4-6 minutes. Then simmer covered until cooked, about 30 more minutes.

4. Mix in iterations: Mix a small portion of warm rice with a small portion of chilled mung beans in approximately 4:1 ratio in volume. Keeping mixing in both in the 4:1 ratio until done.

5. Sauté dry onion flakes in a pan with cooking oil.

6. Serve with sautéed dry onion flakes on top of mung bean coated sweet rice on plates.

Chapter 9 Ingredients

In this chapter, I list ingredients used in alphabetical order, except those which are easy-to-find such as soy sauce, white onion, cilantro, and green onion.

For each ingredient, I include the English name so it's easy to cross reference when you are ready to try a recipe. For ingredients with packaging, I include a picture of the packaging where I use arrows to point to the English name, Chinese name (if on the package), and Vietnamese name (if on the package).

I also list any close substitute that can be used in place of that ingredient.

I specifically call out the brand of the ingredient if my mother highly recommends one or I have a strong preference.

If there are different packaging size or weight you find in the stores, I recommend noting the amount required for the recipe or recipes you want to try. For example, if the recipe calls for 1 oz of an ingredient, then opt to buy a 16-oz instead of a 5-lb package.

<u>Chinese Sausage</u> (also known as "Chinese Style Sausage"). My mother recommends the brand "Kam Yen Jan".

<u>Chopped Onion</u> (also known as Dried Chopped Onion Flakes)

Dried Mushrooms. Some packages may say "dried fungi", which is the same if the fungi are in the shape of mushrooms.

Dried Peeled Mung Bean

<u>Dried Shrimps</u>. I prefer "L" for large size so the individual dried shrimps are easier to handle in the preparation step.

<u>Fish Sauce</u>. My mother highly recommends the brand "Three Crabs Brand".

Hsin-Chu Rice Stick – Thin Kind

Mung Bean Sprouts (Close Substitute: Bean Sprouts)

Perilla (Close Substitute: Mint Leaves)

Pho (also known as rick stick medium). My mother highly recommends "Three Ladies Brand".

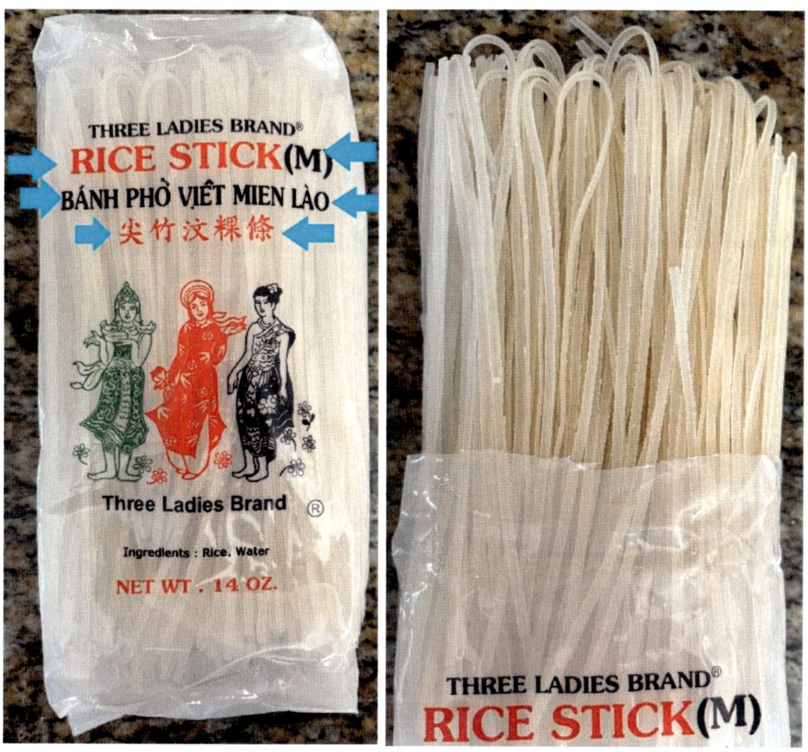

Sugar Peas

Sweet Rice

Vermicelli

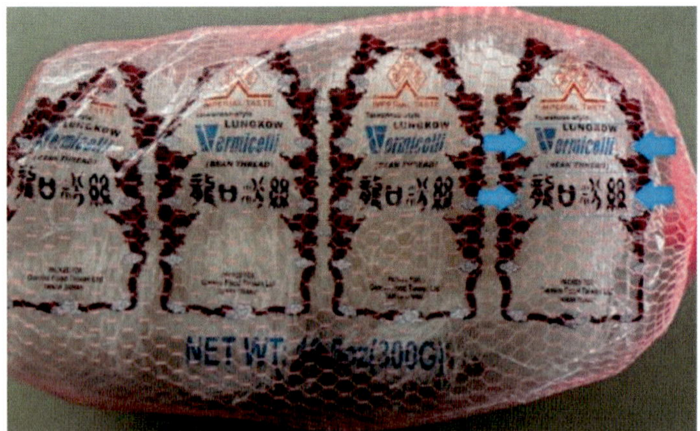

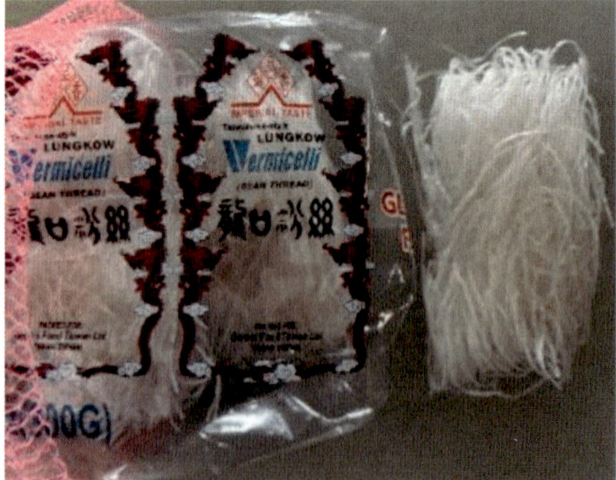

About the Author

After a nearly three-decade technology career in Silicon Valley California, Alan Y Jen retired in 2019. He looked for challenges in retirement, including traveling to all seven continents, eating healthy, and learning his mother's recipes to relive the fond memories of his childhood as well as cooking for his mother in her old age.

As someone who has traveled to over 50 countries and experienced various cuisines, Alan Y Jen wrote this cookbook from the angle of an untrained chef. He carefully observed his mother in cooking each recipe, then attempted each one multiple times until being able to repeat consistently with success each dish.

Made in the USA
Middletown, DE
03 May 2024

53701724R00029